MY BLENDED ROOTS

How to Find Your Spot When You Don't Fit the Mold

BY

JACQUELINE NIDEROST

Dedicated to my two daughters Kendra and Janelle

CONTENTS

CHAPTER ONE

Cassie's Family

Age 9: Grade 4

Cassie, short for Cassandra, was a nine-year-old girl who lived within a small town. Young Cassie was a little clumsy at times, happy, and very adventurous.

Her mother, Joyce, was Cassie's best friend. Joyce worked in technology, and her grandmother was retired. Together, they looked after Cassie.

Joyce had a very professional outlook on life. She was intelligent and focused on Cassie, making sure she was as happy as she could possibly be. She understood Cassie's family on

her father's side was from another country and spoke Arabic, not English. She wanted Cassie to understand her cultural background while they lived in the United States. Joyce knew Cassie's background made her unique and stand out. She also understood it meant questions like "Why do you celebrate Easter like you do?" or, "Why don't you speak Arabic fluently?"

For Cassie, it meant as a young girl, she had the opportunity to juggle two different cultural backgrounds, some first-generation immigrant relatives and, never quite feeling like she perfectly fit into either one of them.

Cassie, like many young girls, wanted to find her style and discover her identity. She tried out many different things to find out what she was good at. Her hobbies included playing soccer, riding horses, and acting.

اللطف

CHAPTER TWO
Standing Out

Age 10: Grade 5

Cassie's mom, Joyce, wanted to make sure Cassie had a happy life full of good experiences. Joyce became a coach for Cassie's local soccer team, helped lead her Girl Scouts troop, and introduced her to the world of stage acting. Joyce was able to balance Cassie's extra-curricular activities with taking care of things at home and working her job in technology.

Cassie was becoming the age where other children would notice and question her differences from the others. Joyce wanted to make sure that Cassie knew about her heritage from the Middle Eastern part of the world. Joyce often played Arabic music at home, but Cassie could never understand what the music meant. Joyce, noticing this, tried to teach Cassie some of the Arabic words. Most of the time, Cassie would say, "Mom, I can't understand a word of what you are saying."

Joyce decided it would be good to enroll Cassie in Arabic language classes. Cassie was eager to join and meet new people. On the first day of class, she entered the classroom and started to look around at the other students. She suddenly felt different – like she was a triangle in a classroom full of circles.

"Hi, this is Arabic class. Maybe you're looking for another class?" said a young girl.

"No, my mom enrolled me. She wants me to learn Arabic," Cassie replied.

"You aren't Arabic!" the girl exclaimed.

"Yes, I am!" Cassie said, "I am Lebanese and American."

"No, you are not! Notice anything? Why don't you look like us? Why?"

"My mom is American, and my dad is from Lebanon," Cassie said.

Just then, the teacher came over. "Enough," she said, "let's welcome all students. There is not just one way an Arabic student should look. We are here to learn the language and the rich cultural heritage we all share, no matter if we are full, half, or a quarter Middle Eastern."

Although Cassie felt at ease with the teacher's comments, she looked around the room and couldn't help but notice she stood out like the triangle among a bunch of circles.

It was break time for the class, and Cassie quickly ran to the lunchroom to get water. "Cassie dear, what are you drinking?" the teacher asked as she entered the lunchroom.

"Um, ice water?" Cassie replied while she looked perplexed the teacher would ask her such a question. "Cassie, why do you put ice in your water? It should be room temperature. Ice can you give you a sore throat," the teacher stated.

Cassie dropped an ice cube back into the glass, replying, "ohhhh...kaaayyyyy," then headed back to class.

When Joyce picked her up, she was upbeat and smiled as Cassie got into the car. "How did it go? Tell me what you learned."

"Well," said Cassie, "I learned that Middle Eastern kids must have a certain hair color, and it must be curly, not light and wavy like mine. Oh, I also learned that ice cubes are not meant to be put in water as it gives you a sore throat, so my question to you is, when will people stop asking me, 'What are you?' I mean, what is your background? And, what in the heck am I supposed to drink when I am thirsty, hot water?" Cassie crossed her arms and was silent the rest of the trip home in the car.

An Awakening at Cultural Day

Cultural Day was right around the corner and Cassie's mom tried to build some excitement around the day. "Cultural day is when you get to show your pride about your background. They have all kinds of fun stuff to do, authentic food, and I am sure you will make friends."

"I bought you a present for the occasion," Joyce said, holding up a shirt inscribed, "I heart Lebanon," written on it.

"Okay, fine," Cassie said. "Thanks, Mom."

The next day, Cassie put on the shirt with her favorite jeans and tennis shoes. They drove to school, and Cassie walked into class. She immediately noticed everyone dressed in traditional Arabic dresses. Her shoulders sank as she let out a deep sigh. "Um, this is Cultural Day, Cassie," one of the girls said. "What are you wearing?"

Just then, the teacher came behind Cassie, put her hand on her shoulders, and said, "Come with me, you left your clothes in the dressing room. This is the Abaya. It is what our ancestors in Lebanon used to wear, Cassie." She held up the long dress. "Put it on. Now, let's get back to the party."

Cassie and the teacher walked down the hall and back to class.

Finding New Alliances

At her middle school, Cassie made a friend named Janelle. Janelle was in the same classroom and often got picked on for having a half-Italian, half-African mixed background. Cassie also got picked on from time to time because of her Middle Eastern mix. The two girls were able to bond easily from having to face the same obstacles with their classmates.

Several times Joyce packed Cassie's lunch with Middle Eastern food. One day at school, Cassie was eating a Middle Eastern sandwich when Rachel, a classmate, shouted in disgust, "Ew, what is that?" When Rachel shouted, all the other classmates turned to see what the commotion was.

"It's called manushe," Cassie replied, a bit confused as to what was wrong with her food. "It's a herb mixed with olive oil that

you put on bread. They eat this in the Middle East."

"No, you are eating a mud sandwich," Rachel argued, "That is so gross!

Everyone, Cassie is eating a mud sandwich!"

The entire classroom began to laugh and make fun of Cassie. She slumped back into her chair, wishing she was invisible at that moment. Cassie stared at the clock wishing for school to end as fast as possible.

The clock struck 3 p.m. With relief, Cassie grabbed her belongings and darted out the classroom door. Cassie nearly made it out of the school when she felt a hand on her shoulder. Cassie spun around to see her best friend, Janelle. Janelle had a mixed background making her a target for her classmates too. Cassie and Janelle had bonded over the fact that they were both treated differently.

"Don't let them bother you," Janelle said. "You know that kids pick on other kids because they don't want to get picked on themselves."

"Doesn't make it hurt any less," Cassie replied.

"Well, who doesn't like a little mud?" Janelle chuckled. "I have tried that now-infamous mud sandwich at your house, and I thought it was pretty delicious."

Janelle put her arm around Cassie and walked home with her.

CHAPTER THREE

The Square Peg in The Round Hole

Cassie arrived home and entered the house with Janelle. Cassie let out a long sigh and said, "I'm making my own lunches from now on," she said to Janelle, then stormed upstairs to her room with Janelle following closely behind. Cassie grabbed a script off her dresser and began reading the lines aloud while pacing in her room.

"Are you preparing for something?" Janelle asked.

"Yes," responded Cassie, "I'm trying out for the school play. There is this character, Isabel, and she is beautiful with blonde, straight hair and fair skin. I really want to play her."

"Um, well, there's just one issue with that, Janelle began, "you're definitely beautiful, but you're not a blonde, straight-haired, fair-skinned girl. Other than that, I think you would be perfect!"

CHAPTER FOUR
Rejection

After class the next day, Cassie went with Janelle to the school drama room. It had rows of seats before an enormous stage where the drama often put on theater productions.

Joyce wanted to support Cassie's acting ambitions, so she hired a local talent manager named Rae. Cassie and Joyce sat down with Rae for their first meeting in the school drama room. "Honey, what is your background?" Rae asked.

"Most people ask me why I am so tan, but really, I am Lebanese-American. I don't tan," Cassie said.

"Okay," Rae said, looking a bit blank and confused in her stare. "We will put 'Italian,'" giving Cassie a warm smile. Cassie sighed, then said, "okay," as if she were used to accepting a stereotype.

Cassie asked her mom on the way back from the meeting, "I do not see what is so difficult about being from a mixed background in acting. It seems like there are certain backgrounds that they get while others, not so much. I wonder if every tan person out there is just 'Italian.' Why is this so hard?" she asked her mom.

"Cassie, there are certain cultural norms people understand and feel familiar with. If you fall out of what someone feels is their 'normal' range of understanding, they can get uncomfortable. Don't let other people's ideas limit you and who you are. Do not take that on and let that define you. The only limit you have in your life is the one YOU place on yourself."

Cassie and Janelle sat down among the other students who were auditioning for the play. When Cassie had a look around, she began to feel nervous seeing all the other girls with blonde, straight hair and fair skin.

"I bet they're all auditioning for Isabel," Cassie grumbled to Janelle.

"Maybe," Janelle encouraged, "just do your best. You practiced so hard for it. I know you'll knock it out of the park."

Over the next hour, many of the blonde girls stood on stage reciting their lines for Isabel while the drama teacher wrote down notes on each of them. Some of the girls really embodied Isabel's qualities. Cassie knew she had some tough competition.

"Will Cassie please come to the stage next?" asked the drama teacher.

Janelle whispered, "Good luck," to Cassie as she stood up and forced her legs to walk forward and onto the stage.

As she looked down at her script, ready to say her first line, an intrusive voice erupted through the room. "Look! It's the mud sandwich girl!" a blonde girl shouted, "She has orange hair now."

All the students in the room began to laugh hysterically leaving Cassie's nerves more heightened than ever before. She began to shake and there was an obvious quiver in her voice as she read her lines. She could barely get through them.

Cassie finished her lines and ran out of the room, bursting into tears.

Cassie received a phone call the morning after her audition. She did not get the part. Cassie was devastated and hid away in her room crying. Ma entered the room and sat beside her on the bed. "What is wrong, Honey?" Ma asked.

"I didn't get the part." Cassie sobbed, "I tried really hard for it."

"Have you thought about all the time you were putting in to make yourself into something you're not?" Ma reasoned. "You can pretend to be certain things like a pirate, or a girl from Holland, but you can't change who you are inside. "You can't change your skin, or your eyes, or how your hair grows. If they don't want to cast a young girl who is beautiful and has rich, mixed ancestry, then you don't need them. Just be you. Instead of pretending to be someone you are not, have you ever tried your hand at soccer? You have practice coming up this Sunday. Your mom is excited to coach your team!" Ma added.

Sunday rolled around, and Cassie reluctantly put on her soccer outfit. Joyce was getting ready for practice too. They drove to the field and began warm-ups. During warm-ups, Cassie lost her balance and tripped over. On her way down, she ended up taking some of her teammates with her.

"Trip over the line in the grass, Cassie?" a teammate sneered.

"Cassie, why don't you play goalie" Joyce suggested. Joyce blew the whistle, and the real game started. Joyce looked over at her daughter to see that Cassie left her goalie post to chase a butterfly. "Cassie, what are you doing? The game is over here!" Joyce said as she signaled to get Cassie's head into the game.

When the game ended, Cassie's team lost. "That's okay," Joyce comforted, "the important thing is you know you did your best."

CHAPTER FIVE

Big Changes for Cassie

Age 11: Grade 6

In the next couple of months, Joyce reconnected with a person at work named George. George, like Joyce, worked in computer technology. There was a common link, and Joyce felt like she could let her guard down with him. Eventually, the two decided to begin dating.

They often enjoyed meals together and would go out and participate in numerous activities

On one date, George suggested to Joyce that he could bring his dog, Piper, to meet Cassie. This would help Cassie warm up to George as well.

Joyce agreed that it was a good idea.

The next day, Cassie could hear Joyce calling her from her bedroom. When Cassie came down, she could see a big, fluffy dog sitting by the front door.

"This is Piper, George's dog. George and I are seeing each other, and he'll be bringing Piper over here to play with you often," Joyce informed Cassie.

"Hi Cassie," George said, "It's very nice to meet you."

"Nice to meet you too," Cassie replied shyly.

"I met George at work, Cassie, do you remember?" Joyce told her. "He was born in South Korea. His mom is from South Korea, and she met his dad when he was in the military. His family moved to Washington State when he was a kid, and he grew up here like me. We have been working in similar fields for a long time."

"Can I take Piper for a walk?"

"I'm sure he would love that!" George replied.

The next few months, Cassie and Piper formed an unbreakable bond. Cassie took Piper on walks every day, and then every night, Piper slept in the bedroom with Cassie. Needless to say, Cassie and Piper were fast friends. Piper was "her dog."

Eventually, Cassie and George started to bond as well. George began driving Cassie to school and taking her to all her extra-curricular activities after school.

One day as George dropped Cassie off for school, she decided to ask George for advice. "How do you deal with bullies and people who are constantly making fun of you because you somehow don't fit into a perfect mold?" I am kind of confused about who gets to create "the perfect mold to begin with."

"That's a good question," George replied, "you know, when I was your age, I got bullied a lot too. When I lived in a small town in South Korea, I was the only half-Korean kid in my school. My features were a little different than the rest of the kids. My hair was dark brown when everyone else had black hair. The other kids excluded me from playing with them because I looked a little different than they did. The parents would look at me with such an inquisitive look on their faces—kind of like trying

to figure out a science experiment of something."

"Then when my family moved to the United States, I wore glasses and liked to play video games, so some kids in my class would call me a nerd and geek. They would throw paper airplanes at the back of my head and never stop. Then I went to school in the United States, and those kids couldn't wait to make fun of my shoes which were from South Korea. They had little anime characters on them, and I quickly learned boys here don't wear shoes with anime characters."

"Needless to say, when you are a child who has one or both parents who are first-generation immigrants here in the US, you can't feel like a kid without a country. You never can seem to perfectly fit into one of them. For me I wasn't Asian enough in South Korea, nor did I look like a typical American of European descent. So, I didn't fit the mold as well. My favorite question was, "what are you?"

"Then, as I got older, I had to deal with a lot of Asian stereotypes others had of me. People would always assume I was a bad driver or I didn't know how to speak English well.

Some people would ask me questions like, "do you like Chinese or Vietnamese food?"

"It was kind of an attempt to connect with me. I didn't have the strength at times to point out there are many different Asian cultures. I just rolled with it at times, "yep I love Chinese food," said George.

"When I tried dating in high school, sometimes girls would go out with me because I didn't look like everyone else. I guess it was flattering but a little creepy. When I met their parents, some would speak loudly and slowly to me – like they were helping me understand what they were saying. I would reply back to them in perfect English. I guess if you don't fit the mold on the outside, some people assumed I was from a different country and didn't speak English."

"Years later, I often wonder if they expected something different from dating a half-Korean guy? In the end, I just wanted to see a movie, go to prom, and looked forward to college. It turns out we actually had way more in common, but we were focused on someone's appearance initially."

"I never had the confidence to stand up to them, so I decided that I needed to change. I decided to be proud of myself and told all my classmates that I don't mind the things that make me different or uncool. Life would be boring if everyone was the same, looked the same, had all the same skills and talents."

"Embrace your uniqueness. Feel sorrow for those narrow-minded people, as they will miss out on all of the greatness that diversity brings to the table. They'll never get to know the beauty of others' uniqueness, their culture, new things that are a wonder to experience. When you are just trying to fit into a mold as a youth, you will find it a blessing to be unique in your way as an adult," George told Cassie.

"Trust me—your time will come. This includes your appearance, food you eat, languages you speak, even the music that you listen to. As you get older, you will want to stand out, and your background makes you unique. It is when you get older you realize there is no mold of the ideal person. Everyone's unique features, hair color, foods you eat from another culture make our country fun and interesting."

"Never let your worst hecklers get the best of you. They are afraid. They get scared when they are introduced to new things. Remember when you were little, and you were afraid to try that new dish that your parents wanted you to try?" George said.

"And remember when you took that first bite and it was wonderful? Well, you will run into those that are afraid to experience new things. Remember what people don't understand, they often fear it and try to make it about you when it is their own insecurities. Don't buy into people's negative words and actions, especially when they are hurtful. Some people ask questions when they are trying to understand something. Others will try and make you feel like the issue is with you. It's not about you."

"Find the humor in things. A little bit of humor can overcome the fear that others may be facing. When kids tease you about the language you speak, the food you eat, the clothes you wear, embrace it and show your pride. I had the best time embracing the stereotypes. I even corrected some of them which were not correct. Why? In the end, it didn't matter. Even when I corrected them, I was showing I was smarter than the bullies were. Intelligence wins in the end," George noted.

"I wish I knew what I know now about my future. I would have worried less, knowing that my future friends would embrace me for all my uniqueness. They would ask me questions about how it was growing up in a multi-cultural environment. They would ask me what it was like to speak a different language at home. They would envy me for knowing more than one language or eat different foods feeling like they missed out. They would be my true friends."

"Oh, one more really important point. Things get better. It gets better in middle school and high school—even better in college! College is wonderful because people are more open-minded and you get to meet all kinds of people, even from around the world. College is all about exploring all of the unique things about a melting pot of people, each who are just as unique as you are. And you will find a whole new group of friends. Friends that are not as superficial as grade school. These are friends that you make for life and care about you for who you are, not what you look like, language you speak, or the foods that you like. Trust me—ethnic food is huge when it comes to college time."

"There is only one you, and that what makes you unique and special. Can you imagine how boring things would be if everyone were the same? That wouldn't be fun at all! You wouldn't learn about new things from other parts of the world, and you would just eat the same old food and same clothes. Boring! That is why the differences in people are so important. We can all learn new things from each other and don't forget to teach your friends some things that they didn't know about you!"

"The United States is a mosaic. Think of a painting; it's beautiful and diverse with lots of different colors. How boring would it be if the painting was all just one color?" George asked.

"And you know what, if I didn't play video games when I was young, I probably wouldn't have found an interest in computer technology and never met your mother."

Cassie felt very warm hearing George's advice. Cassie went into the school that day, and when another girl called her a mud-eater, she stood up for herself.

"I don't need to make fun of others to fit in," Cassie shot back, "At least I have a diverse background and have different things about me that make me unique. What do you have? Cassie asked? Blonde hair like a thousand other girls in the school? You should celebrate differences, not belittle them."

"I'm sorry," the blonde girl apologized. "I guess I didn't think of it like that. Maybe you can tell me more about where you're from?"

"Well," Cassie started, "my heritage comes from Lebanon. In Lebanon, everyone has darker skin, brown eyes. And different types of food grow over there, so we eat different things."

Cassie educated the blonde for the entire recess, and instead of bullying her, she seemed to have warmed up to Cassie quite well.

For the first time, Cassie actually felt happy to be who she was.

One year later, Cassie soon received some good news from her mother. She was getting married.

She remembered the stories her mother would tell her about the many different forms of families; there is no one family that is the right one. "Your family was you, Ma, and I. Now we will have George in the family," Joyce said.

"After we get married, we are going to have a child," Joyce told Cassie, "which means your dream of being a big sister will come true!"

Cassie growing older and having dealt with many biological and cultural differences in her life, began to become very interested in genetics. She eventually found herself taking online computer courses about biological sciences in genetics. She wanted to know why and how genetics made people look different. She could tell you why some babies are born with green eyes or are born with blue eyes. Over time, she became very expert about genetics in a way no one else she knew was. It was her niche.

CHAPTER SIX

The Wedding

The wedding with Joyce and George was a small but beautiful ceremony. Cassie was to serve as maid of honor to her mother.

"Can you help me with my hair, Cassie? "Joyce asked. Cassie began carefully placing the hair pieces in an elegant design. "It's almost time, sweetheart. You should go get ready to take your place at the altar.

Cassie wished her mother good luck and got ready to stand at the altar in support of her mother. The attendees took their places in the rows of pews before falling silent. The traditional wedding music began to play as Joyce wanted into the chapel. Cassie stood like the stoic bridesmaid she was. She held a small bouquet of flowers, wearing her long, black dress with silver shoes.

During the ceremony, when her mom and George began to say their vows, Cassie was overwhelmed with emotion. She was so happy for her mother that she could feel her eyes become moist before droplets started to run down her cheeks.

That was it. Cassie's mom was officially married!

There was a great, big celebration after the wedding ceremony. Dancing, platters of food, and perhaps the biggest cake Cassie had ever laid eyes upon.

When the wedding was over, George moved in. George liked technology and video games and didn't mind sharing junk food every now and then with Cassie. Cassie started to think about all the things that would be different.

"Child," Ma stated, "Have you been holding back from attending events because you think you didn't fit the mold? I find people create their own mold for a family. Instead of trying to fit the mold, you should focus on breaking the mold. I told you there are many different definitions of a family. Just be you.

CHAPTER SEVEN

Cassie's Family Expands Again

"Cassie, you have to call me an ambulance!" Joyce stammered, "George is at work and I'm going into labor!"

"Oh my god, mom," Cassie replied with worry, "just hold on!"

About nine months earlier, Joyce shared the good news with Cassie that her little sister was on the way. Joyce announced her pregnancy. Over the months, Cassie noticed her mother's belly grow larger and larger. Somehow, Joyce managed to stay actively working and juggling her multiple priorities. Now, the baby was arriving.

The ambulance arrived and put Joyce on board as they checked her vitals. Cassie sat beside her mom, holding her hand as they were transported to the hospital.

"The big day is here," Joyce said, smiling at Cassie.

Cassie was both excited and terrified.

Upon arrival to the hospital, Joyce was escorted to the delivery room where she was about to give birth.

Cassie was made to wait outside the room. Anxious, she paced back and forth down the hallway, waiting for any news.

George arrived and hugged Cassie. "I'm so glad you were there for your mom," he told her.

A nurse poked her head out of the delivery room. "Cassie, George, we're ready for you."

Cassie and George entered the room. There she was! A beautiful baby girl. Blonde hair with Asian eyes; certainly, unique features. I guess she won't be fitting into any cookie-cutter version for what a mixed Asian, Arabic child should look like, Cassie thought. Cassie was going to teach her little sister how to handle being in a world where everyone wants to put you in a box. She was going to teach her little sister how to be proud of who she was.

"What will her name be?" Cassie asked.

"Kaia. Her name is Kaia." Joyce said, crying with happiness to hold her second daughter for the first time.

Cassie slept in the hospital room with her mom that night. She didn't want to leave Joyce's or Kaia's side.

She stared at little Kaia as she slept. "I'm going to teach you how to…just be you."

Being true to yourself is one of the most important things you can nurture in life. It's important to live your life in a way that reflects who you are. If you try to be someone or something you're not, you'll sooner or later run into problems because you're ignoring huge parts of yourself that require attention. Just be you.

ABOUT THE AUTHOR

Jacqueline grew up in Sunnyside, WA. She is a proud graduate of Washington State University and the Thunderbird School

of Management. As an adult, she has worked in technology for the past two decades. She continues to love traveling and learning about different cultures, history, and their indigenous cuisines.

The inspiration for writing this book was her two daughters. Her eldest daughter's heritage is Lebanese and Irish. Her youngest is a mix of Korean, German and Irish. Jacqueline has noticed the questions about her children's backgrounds that have come up over the years as they were growing up. Questions from people who are trying to figure out their backgrounds because they don't look the majority of the population or, from one particular culture. While curiosity is normal, she decided to put pen to paper so other youth could see at an early age it is ok "not to fit into any mold," uniqueness is a gift, and she hopes the youth of today can simply focus on being the best version of themselves